MW00787462

BRAND YOURSELF BEFORE SOMEONE ELSE DOES!

Creating a Brand Story That Gets Told Even When You're Not in the Room!

Andrea Oden

Copyright © 2023 Andrea Oden

All rights reserved.

ISBN: 979-8-9880086-0-6

Dedication

I have been blessed with having worked alongside the best of the best. To the tribe I spent 20 years as an HR professional with, I salute you. You gave me the wings to fly. FOR THE LAST TWENTY YEARS, I have had the extraordinary privilege of working alongside some of the most capable leaders in both Corporate America and the Kingdom of God. I've worked with CEOs, vice presidents, directors, managers, and supervisors who have all taught me some truly great lessons about leadership. You have no idea how much you have all taught me about serving and leading with a loving heart. I've also had the honor to serve, sit at the feet of, and learn from some of the world's greatest pastors, teachers, and church staff members. This book is from my heart to yours, with great love and admiration!

Contents

Acknowledgments

There are people in our lives whose encouragement, partnership and support make not only our careers but our dreams possible! To all the teams I have had the pleasure of partnering with over the last twenty years, you have helped make this book possible. To my tribe—those who have allowed me into your lives and careers, it has been my honor to coach, mentor, encourage, and serve you. You have made me dream bigger and so much better. To my amazing parents, who have always provided a safe place for me to just be me. To my brothers (Pete, Leon & Nathaniel), my first and best friends, I love you more than any words I could ever write.

Adrena Stubberfield, my sister, my confidante, my prayer partner, my friend. This book would never have happened without those Thursday evening sister discussions.

Lastly, to every person along my journey who didn't "get" me, didn't understand me, rejected me . . . THANK YOU. This book is truly a result of your part of my story. I wouldn't change a thing!

Welcome to Your Brand Story Journey

If you are reading this book, it's because you are looking to grow your career. Congratulations on this bold move. As a 20+ year leadership and career strategist, I want to tell you, you have done what most people won't do. You have invested in your future.

In this book, we will explore the concept of "branding yourself" and how to create a unique brand story that will help you stand out in your industry. We'll look deeper at what it means to be a brand, why branding is essential, and the strategies and tactics you can use to create an authentic, compelling brand story that will get you noticed.

We'll also discuss how to use social media to promote your brand and craft a personal mission statement that expresses the essence of who you are and what you want to accomplish. Finally, you'll learn how to build relationships with key influencers in your field.

Along this journey, you will hear stories of people just like you and the challenges they faced trying to grow a career and build a solid brand story. You will also read some stories of people who failed to take this step and consequently saw their careers stall out.

You will also hear a few of my own career stories. You will learn about the brand story that was created for me, and then you'll see the brand story I created for myself.

This book is called Brand Yourself Before Someone Else Does because you will find that the world is full of people creating and telling stories. We all tell everyone else's story every day. Think about how many you tell about people you don't know—celebrities, politicians, etc. You also tell stories about the people you *do* know. You tell the brand story of that crazy coworker, the difficult boss, the smart but lazy employee, etc.

You may not realize it, but a story is already being told about you. People are talking about you in your industry and probably beyond it. The question becomes—do you want to control that narrative or give that power to someone else?

The stories people tell about you and your career brand can propel you into a bright future or keep you in the shadows. This book is your guide to creating a powerful, authentic brand story that will help ensure you always control how people perceive your career success.

It's time to take control of the narrative and brand yourself before someone else does.

Are you ready to begin this journey? Let's get started!

Where My Brand Story Began

If I'm honest, and I am, I spent many years of my career doing all the wrong things. I spent years pretending it was okay to be late to work and undependable. I finally figured out the attendance problem one day when a boss took me aside and asked me why I thought it was okay to be late or a no-show. She was not nice in her approach and ended the conversation by telling me if I was late one more time or failed to show up for work again, I shouldn't bother to come because I wouldn't be welcomed back.

From that fateful day, I changed my work habits and put a lot of effort into not just being on time but also striving to be an exemplary employee. This one shift was a career game-changer.

I often tell the story of my very first promotion. I was up for a promotion, and the decision came down to two other candidates and me. The hiring team was sitting in a conference room when the Sr. Vice President entered the room and asked what they were up to. They told him about the three candidates and that they were struggling to make a decision. He looked at my resume and said, "She's the one." When asked why, he replied with one word: "Dependability." He then continued, "I don't know what she knows, but that girl comes to work every day. She's the first one in the building, and she makes a damn good first pot of coffee every morning."

Now I'm not sure which was more important, the dependability or the coffee, but this was a far cry from me being on the verge of being fired for being late. Needless to say, I got the promotion. My brand story was speaking in a room I wasn't even in.

I wish that was the start of a brand story that continued to soar. It wasn't. I was promoted but remained stuck at that level for almost three years. During those three years, I trained three different bosses. You read that right. I trained my bosses. In fact, when boss number two left, I was the interim manager for six months while the company "waited" for my new boss to complete her one-year in-role requirement so she could be relocated and promoted into the manager role. Now don't get me wrong, manager number three was an amazing boss, and it was she who taught me the importance of a brand story. Her brand story was the first one I saw in action.

My Boss's Brand

My new boss arrived on the scene. She was about four years younger than I was and had less tenure with the company, but she had something I didn't. She had a tribe, a mentor, and a sponsor. We'll talk more about that later.

She had also been intentional about her brand.

The first time I heard her tell her story, I realized that she wasn't just about getting the job done; she was out to build relationships and become a trusted advisor. From the moment she arrived on the scene, every meeting she went to, every person she talked to, and every project she worked on, was an opportunity to tell her story and build trust. She was polished, poised and had a career plan that was intentional, deliberate, and well-executed.

From the moment I heard her story, I knew what needed to change in my life and career. From then on out, it became a priority to be intentional about my story and ensure I was proactively positioning myself to be successful. Instead of just working hard, I worked hard *and* made sure that my story was heard and told by the right people.

This amazing leader laid the foundation for my entire career. JBT, if you're reading this, I salute you and hope I've made you proud!

This Book Is About You

This is a book about you. Every page, every paragraph, and every word is designed to get you to see yourself. This book is your assignment, your guide, helping you create a continuous story about your future self. To do that, we must look closely at who you are today. As we do, we will decide who you want to be in 12 months, five years, and beyond. You will begin to learn how to tell a story that is uniquely designed by you and about you. This story will follow you into every meeting, show up on every zoom call, and linger in every room long after you're gone. This story will be told by everyone who interacts with you. And every year, the story will become better and better. This story is about a legend. It is your brand story.

Taking Ownership of Your Career

For many of us, our career is something we take for granted. We assume that just showing up year after year, doing our job, and not rocking the boat is enough. We think if we do great work, our work will speak for itself. Sadly, this is not true. It's not enough to simply do great work. We must also take ownership of our brand story. To do this, we need a strategy.

Your brand story needs to be something you live and breathe every day; it's an ongoing process of self-examination, reflection, and improvement. You must ask yourself difficult questions about your skills, talents, goals, ambitions, and values and how you want the world to perceive you in each stage of life. This is the foundation upon which you will build your brand story. By taking the time to understand who you are today and who you want to become tomorrow, you can create a brand story that is uniquely yours - one that will set you apart from the competition. And, with a brand story that stands out and is authentic to you, you will be able to build a successful career while living a life of purpose.

So let's get started! Ready to craft your brand story? It's time to show up as the leader of your own destiny. Your brand story starts . . . now. Let's go!

Your Career, Your Journey, Your Control

Many of us assume that if we show up to work every day and do good work, we will be rewarded, and our careers will progress. But this is not true. We often think that our work should speak for itself. I'm the first one to tell you that your good work doesn't speak loud enough, and sometimes it isn't noticed at all. Your excellent work can be overshadowed by someone who is not as talented but has something you don't have. You may be dependable and show up to work every day without fail. But you can still be overshadowed by a less reliable person who hasn't been with the organization as long, even if they have a poorer work ethic. You could have more degrees than a thermometer, yet others with less education and less experience may move ahead of you. How does this happen? How do others with less to offer manage to get ahead of you in their career journey? They have a better brand, and they are able to tell a better brand story.

When you create a brand story of yourself, you take control of your career path and prepare yourself for future opportunities. The right brand story puts you in the driver's seat, and you control the acceleration. You have the power to create a career path that is right for you. With your brand story, you show your current and even future employers who you are and what makes you unique. The right brand story gets told repeatedly, and just like the stories about the "big fish," the story gets bigger and better over time. Your brand story gives you a voice in a room crowded with job candidates, performance review discussions, and promotional opportunities—it sets you apart from the competition and propels you to the front of every great opportunity.

Your brand story is about you and your unique journey; it's a narrative that sets your success in motion! You have the power to design a career path of accomplishment and achievement, so go ahead and take control of your future today! Your brand story starts . . . now. Let's get going!

Chapter 1
What are they Saying When you Leave the Room?

"Your brand is what other people say about you when you're not in the room."
~ Jeff Bezos

Meet Cassandra

In my first role as a manager, I had maintained my brand and talked about brand strategies so much that my business partners asked me to do a training series on personal branding. I created this fun six-week training for 25 supervisors and four managers called Brand You! On the third week, we did an exercise that required six leaders to anonymously provide 4–5 descriptive words about each leader. This provided every leader with diverse perspectives on their brand identity. I gathered all of the feedback forms, placed them in unmarked envelopes, and sent them to me. Then, my mission was to compile the responses into a memo I could share in individual meetings with each leader, revealing how their colleagues viewed their professional image.

All was going well until I got to Cassandra. Cassandra had been promoted into her role about six months prior from a front-line position. The first anonymous envelope used adjectives like smart, nice, and interesting. Not really the adjectives I was looking for, so I opened the next envelope. I saw the words promiscuous, slut, and shameful. I quickly tore into the third envelope. The first three words were: tramp, slut, and promiscuous. The next three envelopes revealed more of the same.

I will forever be grateful that I had the good sense to have the envelopes returned to me.

During a meeting with the Operations Director, I tried to ask questions about Cassandra without sharing the feedback. The director invited two managers into the discussion and advised them that I wanted to know their professional opinions about Cassandra. The two managers looked at each other, laughed, and said, "Well, we all know what Cassandra is like."

Meeting With Cassandra

During the meeting with Cassandra, I tried to diplomatically share the feedback. I asked her what adjectives she would use to describe her professional brand. Cassandra thought she was smart, funny and friendly. When I asked her what she believed her peers thought about her, she was momentarily quiet and then said, "Most people like me. I do my work, and I work hard for my team."

When I began to share some of the anonymous comments, Cassandra began to cry. She told me she had been involved in intimate relationships with several employees when she was a front-line employee, but it had been many years before she became a supervisor. Cassandra had no idea what people were saying about her when she was not in the room. She had no idea what "signature fragrance" lingered in every room years later.

What About You?

When you leave the room, what do people say about you? Do they remember your name? Your accomplishments? Your presence?

What happens when you leave the meeting? What happens when the Zoom call ends?

Are you making a lasting impression? Are people talking about your work ethic, intelligence, or passion for success? Do people remember you not only for what you said but how it made them feel?

Are people talking about you being late again? Do people talk about missed deadlines or your negative attitude?

Every encounter, whether it's a meeting or a conference call, leaves an impression. For every email you send out with your name at the top of the page, there is an immediate feeling that follows.

At evening dinner tables, you are being talked about. Best friends know who you are. Husbands and wives talk about you before they drift off to sleep.

Does that sound strange? Think about conversations you've had about your micromanaging boss, the crazy coworker, or the peer who dresses a little too provocatively. Think about the boss you love. You talk about her constantly at home. Your work BFF, you talk about her so much, even if your family hasn't met her yet, they know who she is. Work husbands and work wives become so important we talk about them just like they're real family.

That's why your brand story starts and ends with what they say when you leave the room. What do people say about you? It's a powerful question because it matters more than you think.

Your brand story is the narrative people talk about when you are not present. It doesn't matter if it's positive or negative; your job as is to craft that conversation in a way that reflects well upon your name and image. Control your reputation by carefully crafting how others discuss you—make sure they're always saying good things! Yes, there will be people who don't like you, don't value you, and don't want to work with you. In life, some may attempt to taint your reputation. You have the ability to make sure that any negative remarks about you will never go unchallenged; when someone speaks ill of you in a room, others should be ready and willing to share stories of how amazing and influential you really are. It all starts with having a strong brand image that showcases who you truly are as an individual.

Are you making a lasting impression? Are people talking about your work ethic, intelligence, or passion for success? Do people remember you not only for what you said but how it made them feel?

What do THEY say about YOU when you leave the room? Your success depends on it. Now let's get out there and make a lasting impression!

Are you ready for the challenge? Make sure those conversations match up with who YOU want to be known as. Take charge of YOUR brand story today! You have the power to make it happen, so don't wait any longer. Start creating the story that you want people to remember you for!

Make sure that when you leave the room, they remember your name and your impact with admiration. That's how you build an inspiring legacy. What do THEY say about you when you are not in the room? It's time to find out. Make sure they're saying something positive. Now, let's get started on making sure your brand story is one that will be remembered forever!

Are you ready to take charge of YOUR brand story? Let's get started and make sure it ends with something inspiring. What do THEY say when you leave the room? Let's find out and make sure it is something worth remembering! Get ready to take charge of YOUR brand story today! Let's create a legacy worth remembering. You have the power to make it happen, so don't wait any longer. Let's go!

Let's make sure they remember your name and your impact with admiration. It all starts with what YOU do and say. Create an inspiring legacy that will be remembered forever. Let's get started now! It all begins when you ask yourself: What do THEY say about me when I leave the room? You have the power to shape that conversation—are YOU ready for the challenge? Let's go!

Now that we've seen a few brand stories in action, let's go back and define a brand.

Chapter 2
What is a Brand?

"A brand is a voice and a product is a souvenir."
~ Lisa Gansky

What is a brand? According to the American Marketing Association (AMA), a brand is a "name, term, sign, symbol, or design, or a combination of them intended to identify the goods and services of one seller or group of sellers and to differentiate them from those of competition".

In terms of your career, your brand is how you present yourself to others.

What is a career brand?

Career branding is about managing your name and your reputation. Your career brand directly reflects who you are as a person. It's what someone else would say about you if you weren't in the room. It motivates you, pushes you to achieve new levels, and shows your commitment. Your brand showcases your core values in life as well as your strengths and weaknesses. Your career brand is what I like to call your "signature fragrance" that lingers in the room long after you're gone.

What do others say about you when you're not in the room?

How do people feel about working with you?

Do others enjoy working with you, or does the thought of working with you garner feelings of exhaustion, fear, or anxiety?

What automatic emotion do people feel when they realize they have to work with you?

What automatic emotion do others feel when your name comes up in conversation?

What do people "feel" about your level of work, commitment, and follow-through?

Are you the first choice for the next promotion or project?

These are all questions to consider as you think about your career brand. Your career brand should be strong enough that people would still recognize it if you were to leave the room. Your career brand should be so strong that people know who they're talking about when they describe you—without even using your name.

Your brand is not just about your skills and education; it's also about how others perceive you. You may be thinking to yourself, "my work should speak for itself." Let me be the first to tell you—it doesn't. Your work doesn't tell the story of your brand. Your work doesn't tell the story of what you stand for, who you are and how you interact with others. Your brand tells a story, and your work starts but doesn't finish it. Your brand is the story that surrounds your work, your reputation and your attitude. Your brand is the emotion others feel when they think of you, interact with you, talk about you, and work with you.

Your brand should reflect the kind of person you are and the values that guide your life. You don't have to be perfect, but authenticity is key. Your career brand must represent who you really are and what you stand for. It's not about being someone else; it's about being the very best version of yourself.

Your career brand is your calling card, and it's up to you to ensure it resonates with those who come into contact with it.

There's a cool saying that says when you start out on your career journey, it's all about your work. But as you progress, your career becomes more about your relationship with people.

Your Work vs. Your Brand Story

One argument with a coworker, one frustrated outburst in a meeting, or one email sent off-hours when you're tired can create your brand story and ruin years of great work.

You could be in your career for years and do great work but never be recognized because you either haven't established a brand or your brand has been damaged. And it's easy to damage a brand and erase your work. Now, let's be clear; bad stories have a much longer shelf life than good ones. When you allow your work to speak, it tells only part of your brand story. Your ability to do your work and do it well is about how well you have been educated and trained and how you have developed your skills.

Your brand story, on the other hand, is about how you interact with people and how they perceive you. It's about being proactive in developing relationships and proactively telling your story. Your career brand is more than just a list of experiences or accomplishments. It's what stands out and makes you unique in a world filled with people with the same skills, education, and training as you.

Your brand story should represent who you are and what you stand for. Its narrative binds your work together and presents it compellingly—to be shared with others, especially those in positions of influence. Your brand story is the emotion behind how you do your work, how people feel when they interact with you, and the impression your work makes on those around you. Your brand story is what sets you apart from everyone else.

Your career brand should be strong enough that people would still recognize it if you were to leave the room. When done right, your career brand will build credibility and trust with your current organization, potential employers, your peers, collaborators, and friends. It should be so powerful that people can accurately identify who you are—even without seeing your work.

Your work and your brand story need to collaborate to create a powerful, lasting impression. Your work is the foundation of your career success and can contribute significantly to your brand story. When done well, both will allow you to achieve the success you deserve in your career.

This means taking the time to craft a story that tells who you are, what you stand for, and why your work matters—something that makes people want to invest in you and your career. Your brand story is the best way to ensure that all your work is not forgotten or overlooked and that you are remembered for your talent and accomplishments.

If you believe your work should speak for itself and that your work is more important than any story, let me give you a few examples of genius work destroyed by out-of-control brand stories:

Roseanne Barr — In May of 2018, comedienne Roseanne Barr made one move that destroyed her brand, and she paid the ultimate price of being fired. One tweet was enough to cancel her show and ruin relationships with many close colleagues.

Kanye West — While he may be a musical genius, many say his public behavior is destroying his reputation, and now, many companies refuse to work with him. At the writing of this book, eleven companies have ended their affiliation with Kanye West, and many brand experts say his recent comments and behavior far outweigh his musical genius.

Matt Lauer — Former Today Show host Matt Lauer's brand was destroyed after sexual misconduct allegations against him surfaced in 2017. After the scandal, he was immediately fired from NBC and has struggled to rebuild his brand ever since.

Bill Cosby — The comedian was seen as America's Dad for decades. But then allegations of rape and sexual assault surfaced against him in 2014. Over the years, his established brand quickly crumbled, and his reputation was damaged so severely that his work would forever be tainted.

Paula Deen — In 2013, the celebrity chef was found guilty of racial discrimination, and her reputation suffered a devastating blow. Her brand quickly lost its luster as many companies that had previously worked with her backed away. Paula Deen's partnerships went running for the hills after the infamous "Butter Queen" admitted to using racial slurs in the past.

These examples show how quickly and drastically a person's brand story can affect their career. As you can see, your actions have the potential to make or break your career, so it's important to take charge of your narrative and craft one that showcases your work in the best light possible.

The lesson here is clear: brand yourself before someone else does. You must understand that how you manage your brand will determine whether people perceive you as an asset or a liability. There are countless ways to create, build, and manage your personal brand—it all starts with being aware of the type of image you want to present to the world. As Nike says, "Just do it!" Start making moves today to establish and maintain a positive professional brand for yourself!

Chapter 3
Benefits of a Brand Story

"Create the highest, grandest vision possible for your life because you become what you believe."
~ Oprah Winfrey

Your brand story is the "story" speaking for you. It's who you are and what you stand for. Your story is the heart and soul of who you are. Constructing your career brand begins and concludes with narrating your story. It is these experiences that have shaped who you are today. Your career brand story is your childhood and all of its glee—and also its traumas. Your brand story is defined by the lessons you've learned and how they have shaped your values and beliefs. Once you begin to understand who you are and the story that defines you, you can communicate it to the world. Not only that, but the world around you will also know who you are and what you bring to any career table.

Why Build a Career Brand Story?

Let's go back for a moment and visit the Oprah Winfrey Show. Before the show was called simply Oprah, it began its story as A.M. Chicago, a half-hour morning talk show. On January 2, 1984, Oprah began her journey as the host. Within one month, the show moved from last place to first place in Chicago's ratings. In 1985, the name of the show became the Oprah Winfrey Show, and it ran for 24 seasons, ending with a final show on May 25, 2011.

Year after year, the show would take a summer break before coming back for fall. Each autumn brought its own unique theme and new set design, and Ms. O's wardrobe was even refreshed regularly!

Just like Oprah Winfrey's show, which returned every fall with new themes and set designs, you can strive to make your professional brand bigger, better, and stronger each year too. But why is building a personal brand so important? Let's take a deeper look.

Famous Brands

What immediately comes to mind when you hear the following names?

- McDonald's
- Nike
- Michael Jordan
- Beyoncé
- Kim Kardashian
- Taylor Swift
- Serena Williams

The minute you read each name, a vision entered your mind. Each of the above brands has been meticulously created. Someone took the time to design, strategize, and communicate the idea they wanted to convey to make a lasting impression. The same goes for your brand. When you intentionally create your professional brand, you can control what people think of when they hear your name. You create the image that comes to mind when people think of you.

Why Is This Important When It Comes to Your Career?

Think for a few minutes about the worst boss you've ever had. What comes to mind? What emotions do you feel?

You immediately thought of a particular experience you had working with this person. Your mind returned to something they did or said that made a lasting impression on you. People remember experiences, especially negative ones. That bad boss invokes a strong emotion when you think about them.

The same goes for your professional brand. People remember experiences and conversations they've had with you. They reflect on your work ethic and how you showed up in meetings. If you create a solid, positive brand, you create the narrative. You get to decide what emotion you want to invoke when people think of you.

Building a career brand that showcases your brand story can boost your career in many ways. Let's consider a few of them.

Increased Visibility

When your brand becomes a compelling story, it automatically increases your visibility. You begin to become recognized as an expert, a subject matter expert. When your story is being told, you become more visible. When people begin speaking your story language, you command attention. The more your story is told, the more visible you become and the more people want to be a part of your story.

When you become an expert in something, your self-confidence increases. You take ownership of the skills and knowledge that you possess, leading to increased confidence in yourself and your abilities. Your reputation becomes known in places far and wide, leading to greater opportunities in your career. Not only that, the world around you will know who you are and what you bring to any career table.

Trust and Credibility

With increased visibility comes trust. People begin to trust that you're an expert in your field, opening up numerous opportunities for career growth, collaboration, networking and mentorship opportunities. Trust is the foundation of relationships, and your career brand helps build that trust. Your credibility will be solidified as people come to recognize you as an expert in your field.

Your story is the bridge between who you are and what you can do, amplifying your trustworthiness.

Building trust makes it easier to build relationships within your current organization. You become a go-to person for your boss, your coworkers, and customers. This adds more credibility to your brand story and enhances your reputation in the professional world.

When people know who you are and what you stand for, they begin to look up to you as a leader in your field. They may even come seeking advice or mentorship, further increasing your credibility and career opportunities.

By developing a strong brand story, you open yourself up to new avenues of success in your professional life. It is the key to unlocking opportunities that may have otherwise been hidden or inaccessible before. It makes you more visible and credible in your field, leading to potential career growth.

When you successfully grow your brand, credibility is the immediate byproduct. After all, as your visibility and reach grow, so does an inherent trust in your expertise. This trust in your brand creates prime opportunities for valuable collaborations, powerful mentorship connections, and priceless networking moments.

Higher Salary Potential

Everyone wants money, and money follows when you have a reputation that commands the attention of other organizations. Money hits the table when you develop a stellar brand, and that story becomes visible and trustworthy within your organization. Why? Because the leaders within your current organization know the value you add to it, and they are afraid to let you go. You become so valuable that they don't want to lose you to another organization. This means that it's raise time! It means salaries at the top of the pay bands. As your brand story gets shared, other organizations see your success, and they will come knocking on your door with even more job offers — all offering money and career enhancement opportunities.

Oprah never settled for being just "good enough." She came back every season with new and inspiring themes and set designs, cementing the success she already had while paving the way for more to come.

And with time and effort, you can do the same for your personal brand. You control what people remember when they hear about your professional brand. Let's work together to make yours stand out within your industry. Let's start building your career brand story!

Chapter 4

It's not your Boss's Job to Grow your Career

"Blaming others is nothing more than excusing yourself..."
~ Robin S. Sharma

We may mistakenly believe that it is our boss's responsibility to raise our career up the ladder or someone else's job to increase and build upon our professional reputation. However, this could not be any further from reality. You might be lucky enough to have a great boss who is a true leader in the sense that they understand how to grow and develop your career and promote a positive image of yourself in the workplace, but more often than not, this is not the case. I'm going to tell you what most people won't. Your boss may not even be capable of helping you grow your career. Not every person who holds a higher title has the capacity to lead you to the next level.

Your boss may be unable to help you grow your career because they lack the experience or knowledge of what it takes to take you to the next level. They may lack the resources and skills to develop and guide you in a positive direction. You might even find that their own goals are at odds with yours or even self-serving. In plain English, your boss may not want you to move to the next level because they may be afraid you will take their job or feel you are so valuable that they can't lose you.

Your boss might also come from a different professional background than where your career could be heading, so there is no guarantee that they will know how to foster growth in your specific field. Moreover, many bosses do not prioritize growth opportunities for their employees as much as they focus on meeting deadlines while chasing profits—so they don't have time or resources dedicated to helping employees like yourself reach their full potential.

Let's face it; your boss has their career to think about. In today's work culture, many leaders are literally fighting to keep their job, particularly at the higher leadership levels.

And . . . it is possible to put your career in the wrong hands.

Meet Tina

When I met Tina, she was on the fast track to her next promotion. She was a brilliant manager, ready to step into a director role. When her boss, Shawn, was promoted to a new position, he immediately made Tina part of the package. Shawn wouldn't take the promotion unless he could bring Tina along. What a great compliment to Tina and her work as a manager! This one comment to higher-level leaders was a massive boost for Tina's brand and reputation.

Tina made the lateral move with a small salary increase but a big promise. "You will be promoted to director in 18 months." Tina knew that Shawn would be promoted soon as he was a brilliant leader with many industry connections.

True to Tina's prediction, Shawn was promoted a year later. However, Tina did not replace Shawn. Instead, another director from a different department was brought in to lead the team. Tina continued in her role as a manager and rarely heard from Shawn after his departure.

This example reveals a powerful lesson—it is not your boss's job to increase and build upon your professional reputation. Your brand story is completely in your hands. It is up to you to invest the time, energy, and resources into cultivating the narrative you want everyone to recognize. You have to be proactive in developing yourself professionally and ensure you consistently make moves toward achieving your goals.

So what happened to Tina?

Tina began to do the work of creating a brand that was independent of her boss. When the new director arrived on the scene, Tina was prepared. She had worked hard to become a thought leader in her field, building relationships with senior leadership across the organization and creating initiatives that propelled her career forward. Ultimately, Tina was promoted to Director—all because she took ownership of her career path.

The moral of the story: It is not your boss's job to grow your career. It's yours. Take control and create the narrative you want to be remembered for! You have the power to make a name for yourself and boost your reputation in the workplace. Put in the effort, stay focused, and never give up on achieving success.

You can do it—Tina did!

Chapter 5
Meet Your Future Self

"Your future self is watching you right now through your memories."
~ Aubrey de Grey

Meet Your Future Self!

I want to take this opportunity to introduce you to someone very powerful. Let me introduce you to a person who is a celebrity in business. This person is someone people want to work with. In fact, people are clamoring to work with them. This person earns top dollar and is the envy of many. This person is you—in the future.

Your future self is a successful, confident, and well-respected individual who has made it their goal to stay ahead of the trends. They have worked hard to develop invaluable skills that will set them apart from the competition. They know how to maximize your talents and use them to achieve great success.

Take a moment and think of your best possible self ten years from now. You are ten years older and have the career of your dreams. You have the title you want and the salary you know you're worth. Maybe you have a family, and you are living in the home of your dreams. Whatever it is, take a moment to envision what this looks like for you. Do you have that image? Now let's make it happen by creating your brand story.

For you to have that life, for you to become your future self, you have to do the work of creating and living that story.

The following exercise will help you meet your future self.

Future Self Exercise

For this exercise, get into a quiet place where you won't be disturbed. You will need a journal or blank document on your computer.

Read each question, close your eyes and write down whatever comes to mind.

At the top of your journal page, write:

My Future Self and today's date

Now answer the following questions/statements:

What is the date ten years from today?

What career do I have?

Where am I working, and what is my job title?

Who am I surrounded with (family, friends)?

What is the most important thing that I will have accomplished ten years from now?

What kind of lifestyle do I have?

What makes me the proudest of myself?

List any other goals that my future self will have reached.

Now, imagine your future self in vivid detail. Really imagine how you will feel, look, and act as your future self. Capture all this imagery in your journal or document with words and pictures.

Take the time to write down everything you can imagine about your future self. This will be a powerful exercise that will help you on your journey to becoming that person. It will also serve as motivation to keep pushing yourself towards success.

Once you have finished this exercise, you will read it regularly. Visualize yourself living out your answers to the questions. Feel powerful and inspired by who you will become ten years from now.

Congratulations! You have just met the most amazing person you will ever know. You have just met your future self!

Now let's create the brand story!

Chapter 6

What's Your Superpower?

"I think every individual has his or her own power, and it's a matter of working, taking time and defining what that power is."
~ Jill Scott

We all have areas where we perform and outperform others continually. Your genius is your superpower, and when used correctly, it can easily catapult your career forward. So how do you understand your superpower?

It starts with knowing yourself. You have to understand what unique skills and talents you bring to the table. But while we often know what we're good at, we don't always know how people need us to use it. A great brand story solves a problem, and you are the solution. Here's how to leverage your genius so that others can benefit and, in turn, make you successful.

You have been solving problems throughout your career. In your personal life, your friends and family recognize your superpower. There are things people come to you for because you are the solution. So let's start this journey with your tribe.

Your tribe are the people who "get" you and value you. They are the first source for understanding who you are and the value your brand provides.

With their help, you can discover your unique superpower and use it to build your career. This simple path to building a powerful brand story involves just a few smart actions:

Reach Out to Your Tribe

The first step in understanding your superpower is to reach out to those closest to you—your tribe. This could include friends, family members, colleagues, mentors, or anyone who knows and appreciates your gifts and talents. I would even say go out on a limb and include your boss as a more senior leader who knows you well. Remember, this is about your career, so your tribe should include people who know you professionally, who have seen your work and who know you well.

In this step, you will send an email to three to five people in your tribe and ask them for honest feedback on your strengths. It might seem like an odd request, but it's the best way to understand your current brand and build your brand story.

Here's a sample email you can use to gather feedback:

Dear Tracy,

I'm currently on a journey to grow my career, and I am beginning by creating a brand that others can trust and depend on. With your help, I'd like to clearly understand how others see me and the value I add. Would you please take a moment and answer the following four questions?

1. What talents do you believe I have that add value to others?

2. When you think of me and my gifts and talents, what would you say are my strengths?

3. What four words come to mind when you think of me?

4. How have you seen me help individuals and teams succeed?

I'd be grateful if you would reply with your answers within the next 48 hours.

Thank you for being such a trusted and supportive friend on my career journey,

Andrea

The answers to these four questions will provide insight into how others view your strengths, which will help shape your brand professionally. Every year, you will "test your tribe" by asking a new group of trusted and supportive friends to describe your brand.

Now that you have gathered feedback from your tribe, let's take the next step and ask your boss about your superpower.

Ask Your Boss

At least once a year, your boss gives you a performance evaluation. It's an excellent opportunity to get feedback on how you're doing and what areas need improvement.

Go back over the last three years and see what feedback you've already received. Make a list of what repeats year after year. Include the specific areas where you do well and make a separate list containing areas of opportunity.

Struggling With How to Ask Your Boss for Feedback?

One of the best ways to ask your boss for positive feedback is to sit down with them and have an open, honest conversation. When you do, express your appreciation for their time and patience and convey your commitment to continued growth and improvement.

Explain:

- What you like about working with them
- How they have helped you learn and grow
- Which areas you would like to focus on in the coming six months

This will show them you are serious about your professional development and genuinely interested in improving. Ask for constructive feedback or suggestions that may help you move forward.

This is a great way to build trust with your boss and gain insight into the areas you need to focus on for improvement. It also shows you are serious about your personal and professional development, which can help bolster your brand.

At the end of the day, having a solid understanding of who you are and what sets you apart from those around you is the key to establishing yourself as an industry leader.

When you understand your superpower and who it brings value to, you can begin building your professional brand. Having an understanding of who you are and how you can make an impact is vital when it comes to using your unique skills to brand yourself as a leader in your industry.

And don't forget that asking your boss for feedback is an important part of this process. It enables you to gain insight into where improvement is needed and what about your performance is valued.

Now that you have gathered feedback from your tribe and your boss, let's take the next step and use it to create a powerful brand story.

It's time to create your brand story!

Chapter 7
A Word About Your Weaknesses

"I didn't go to Harvard, but many of the people who work for me did."
~ 50 Cent, rap artist and entrepreneur

I know some of you may be wondering why we didn't address our weaknesses and only collected feedback on our strengths. It's because when it comes to your brand story, your weaknesses don't matter.

It is often suggested that leaders should strive to strengthen their weaknesses. In fact, many organizations in Corporate America hire individuals based on their strengths and then spend vast amounts of that person's career attempting to improve the areas they are least skilled in.

When it comes to your brand story, focusing on weaknesses can be a mistake. Instead of spending time and energy trying to "fix" our weaknesses, it is more beneficial to double down and focus on areas where we already have strength. Giving most of your energy, attention, and focus to the topics you know well can help you stand out in a way that trying to fix weaknesses may not allow you to.

Of course, this isn't an excuse to ignore areas of improvement or areas where you need growth, particularly when it comes to your character. For instance, if you lack integrity, this is not an excuse to ignore it. This is about what you can hire others to do for you or use software to automate for you.

Ultimately, when it comes to your brand story, understanding and embracing your strengths will help you stand out more than attempting to fix weaknesses. The only thing that happens when you spend time working on your weaknesses is they become less critical weaknesses. When you work on your weaknesses, you may become average at best. And let's be honest; nobody pays for average. No company will promote average. However, if you spend time perfecting your strengths, you can become extraordinary. And that's what people stand in line to pay for. Think Apple's latest iPhone vs. Walmart's Tracfone.

Remember, it's not about being a well-rounded leader. It's about becoming extraordinary at what you're best at. That is the key to building a powerful brand story and carving out your own unique place in the world. So embrace your strengths, focus on them, and make them shine.

Chapter 8
Rediscover Your Genius

"Everybody is a genius. But if you judge a fish by its ability to climb a tree, it will live its whole life believing that it is stupid."
~ Unknown

Rediscover Your Genius

Everyone has unique skills, talents, and abilities that make them who they are. And when it comes to branding yourself professionally, those qualities are invaluable. The challenge most professionals face is that they don't clearly understand their unique superpower.

I call it your "genius." And Albert Einstein has been quoted as saying, "Everybody is a genius. But if you judge a fish by its ability to climb a tree, it will live its whole life believing that it is stupid." Now I don't know if Albert Einstein said these words or not, but they are very true. Everyone has unique gifts, skills, and talents, and everyone has a purpose on this earth.

You are a true genius when you learn to take your talents, skills, passions, and values and put them into action.

We are all born geniuses. Somewhere along the way, we lost it . . . we forgot we are a genius.

So let's rediscover your genius!

When Superpower Meets Genius

You've collected all the responses from your tribe and your boss. Now what?

Take it all in. Really sit down and bask in the responses you received. Read them and enjoy what people have said about you. It's not often you receive such glowing fan mail, so really enjoy it.

This is the beginning of your brand story, the one already being told about you. After you're done basking in your glory, look for patterns:

What themes do you see?

What words or phrases are used repeatedly?

Take out your notebook and write at the top of a clean page:

Superpower Questions

Reread the responses, list each person's name, and identify the keywords or phrases that stood out to you.

The purpose of collecting this feedback is to give you a clear idea of what you are already brilliant at. This feedback is evidence that you have superpowers.

In addition to superpowers, you always have a genius that you were born with. You were created with some unique abilities. This is your God-given genius, and everyone has it. You just need to identify it and nurture it.

The best way I've learned to discover your genius is to take a personality assessment.

In my coaching practice, I have found two great tools that help you define your genius!

DISC Leadership Assessment

I use a uniquely created DISC Leadership Assessment in partnership with the John Maxwell Leadership Team. It is a remarkable brand-building practice for leaders. This assessment grants insight into what naturally drives an individual, revealing their unique strengths and weaknesses for use in their career.

The DISC Leadership Assessment outlines four areas as they relate to your genius:

- Your Key Strengths & Obstacles to Those Strengths
- Your Leadership Strengths
- Your Communication/Collaboration Style
- The Environment Where You Can Do Your Best Work
- The Keys to What Really Motivates You

If you would like more information on DISC, please visit my website www.andreaoden.com/DISC and begin the journey of discovering your genius.

StrengthsFinder Assessment

The StrengthsFinder Assessment is another great tool for leaders to identify their unique skills, traits, and talents. This assessment reveals an individual's natural talents and how to use them in the workplace. It also provides insight into what energizes them and areas that need improvement.

The StrengthsFinder Assessment provides a list of 34 strengths that the team at Gallup identified during 25 years of research and gives you insight into your top five. Highly engaging, articulate descriptions of each strength are provided in the book StrengthsFinder 2.0 by Tom Rath, along with examples of how that strength has been used to create positive results.

For more information on StrengthsFinder, visit Gallop, Inc. at www.gallup.com/home.aspx.

Both the DISC Leadership Assessment and the StrengthsFinder Assessment are great tools for anyone looking to identify their genius and use that knowledge to build and lead an extraordinary brand!

You, my friend, are a genius. Invest in yourself and rediscover your genius. You may be surprised how much your superpower and genius can help you build an amazing brand.

Remember, you are brilliant. Embrace it and share it with the world. Your genius is a gift only you have—don't waste it!

Turn the page, and let's write a beautiful story, the brand called you!

Chapter 9

Your Superpower Purpose Statement (Sps)

"May you live long enough to know why you were born."
~ Cherokee Birth Blessing

Your Superpower Purpose Statement (SPS)

Congratulations on gathering the necessary feedback from your tribe and boss and on discovering your genius through a leadership personality assessment! Now, it's time to start putting all of this information together—creating a narrative that accurately reflects and encompasses your brand story. Let's get started!

Unlock your potential and achieve greater career success with a Superpower Purpose Statement (SPS)! This statement will guide you in defining your passion and talent as well as what you do (and why) for the upcoming year. Creating an SPS helps you remain focused on the principles that drive growth in your professional life.

Your SPS will be the guiding light of your personal brand story as you move into a successful career. Spend some time thinking about what drives you, and use this statement to focus your energy on your goals for the next year. This is your chance to show off who you are and share your unique brand story with the world.

Remember, your brand story sets you apart and allows people to see the real you. So let's take some time, think about it, and create a unique brand story that will guide you for the next 12 months—and beyond!

Begin Thinking of Yourself as a Brand

Beginning today, start thinking of yourself as a living, breathing brand that is unique and powerful. Ask yourself the following questions to get started:

- What are my core values?
- What unique skills do I have that set me apart from others?
- What assets can I bring to any project or company?
- How can I position myself to stand out and be seen as an authoritative leader?
- What unique experience do I bring to any situation?
- How can I use my talents to create something extraordinary for others?
- What emotions do I want people to feel when working with me?
- What do I want people to say about me in every room long after I leave it?

The answers to these questions will help guide your brand's creation. They form the basis of your brand story, which is the story you want to tell and want others to continuously tell about you. Now that you have an idea of your brand, let's take this and put it with the information you received from your tribe and your boss.

**Your Superpower Purpose Statement =
What You Do (Talent) + Who You Are + Why You Do It**

What You Do

The next step is to collect some keywords from all the work you've done so far. Now, go back and look at your list of unique gifts, skills

and talents. Write down 4–5 gifts, skills and talents you have identified. Review the emails from your tribe and your boss detailing the
many ways you add value, and write down all the repeated words or
phrases. List how your tribe repeatedly says you contribute.

This is what you do.

Who You Are

Now, review your DISC assessment or your StrengthFinders report.
What resonates with you? Pull three to five sentences or phrases that
you really loved about your assessment, the things that made you say,
"Yes! That's me!" Now you have several words, phrases, and sentences
that describe your brand.

This is you, my friend, and this is who you are.

Why You Do It

Now it's time to get in touch with the why behind your work. What
is the passion that drives you? Why do you feel so strongly about what
you do? It could be an overall mission or something that motivates
you to keep going.

Now that you know what you do, let's discover why you do it.
When you think about your skills, gifts, and talents, why do you use
them? What drives you to do what you do? In what ways does it
bring you joy? When you reviewed your assessment, what did you
discover about why you do what you do?

When it comes to your why, Simon Sinek, author of *Leaders Eat
Last* says, "People don't buy what you do; they buy why you do it." So
why do you do what you do? This is about the end game.

This is why you do it.

Your Brand Story

Now for the fun part. Take all of that information and write down a
sentence or two summarizing your brand story. Make sure it's vibrant

and relevant and expresses who you are, what you do, and why you do it.

Think of this as your personal motto or slogan. This will be something that you can read over and over again to remind yourself why you do what you do.

Andrea's SPS

My superpower is my ability to help others discover their authentic gifts, talents and strengths to **effortlessly** position them for career and relationship growth so they may live a maximum-impact life. Your abundant life is my passion!

This is taken directly from my tribe and my DISC assessment and ends with my passion.

If you are a marketing specialist, your SPS could sound like this:

My superpower is my understanding of marketing principles coupled with my ability to engage and convert customers with creative strategies to help your business reach its goals. Making a difference in people's lives is my passion!

If you are a human resources professional, your SPS could sound like this:

My superpower is my ability to create an atmosphere of open communication and understanding where employees can produce their best work. Building relationships that help others reach their highest potential is my passion!

If you are a sales professional, your SPS could sound l like this:

My superpower is my ability to build long-lasting relationships that result in sales. Helping others experience success is my passion!

These Superpower Purpose Statements are just guidelines, so feel free to write your own based on what you've learned about yourself and your brand. Remember, this is your brand story and should be specific to you.

Now that you've discovered your brand story, take the time to think about how it influences what you do daily. What principles will help guide you? How can these be applied in all areas of your career and life? The brand story you have discovered will help guide every decision and action, so make sure it resonates with you and stands the test of time.

By discovering your brand story, you are now aware of who you are and why you do what you do. This knowledge can build confidence in yourself and your brand, which will show outwardly.

Remember that every brand is unique, so take the time to focus on what makes you distinctive and remarkable. The brand story you have discovered will serve as your lighthouse, and it's up to you to stay true to who you are.

When you spell out your brand story and commit to living it every day, your career and life will reach new heights. So don't be scared to put yourself out there and let your brand story shine! You have something special to offer the world, so let your brand help you make a mark on it. Your brand story will lead the way!

Chapter 10
Put Your Brand Story to Work for You

"To fulfill your purpose, you must first know and celebrate your identity."
~ T.D. Jakes

Now that you've gone through the hard (but fun) work of defining and creating your brand story, it's time to put it into action. Making your brand story come alive requires effort in three distinct areas:

- Becoming a brand at work
- Growing your brand on social media
- Expanding your brand within your industry

You have created your Superpower Purpose Statement. It needs to be your living, breathing statement every day in the workplace. The more you can show how your brand story is helping you deliver on promises at work, the more valuable and brandable you become. Leverage this statement with colleagues and employers—it's when the "you" brand starts becoming part of the conversation.

Let's look at four ways to become your brand at work. In your current role, you have a brand story to tell; think about ways you can use it to add value.

In your current role, where can you shine bright? Review your emails from your tribe as well as your notes from your performance reviews and your boss. Where do you organically add value? This is what you need to do more of.

When it comes to growing your brand at work, there are four areas to focus on to get your brand story out.

1. Commit by Sharing the Story

You have done the work of creating your brand and your SPS; now, share it with your tribe and your boss. The more you share your brand story, the more you commit to it. This could look like adding a tagline to your emails that tells who you are.

Here are a few taglines to get you started:

"Your Career Brand Strategist..."

"The Leader's Coach..."

"The Sales Mentor..."

"Number 1 Strategy Coach..."

"Million Dollar Recruiter..."

"Top Biller..."

When you commit to sharing your brand story, it comes alive.

2. Recruit Accountability Partners

One of the best ways to commit to your brand and implement it is by assigning accountability partners. Ask two or three people you regularly work with to hold you accountable for your brand story. Share your brand story with them and ask them to hold you accountable whenever you are not honoring your brand. Be very specific: I want to always show up as the brand "XYZ." You will also tell your accountability partners how you want others to feel about working with you. "I want people to feel ABC when they work with me." In my coaching practice, I ask my tribe to share a real-life person. I ask them to provide a real-life person as an example for their tribe. For instance, if you want to show up as Michele Obama, your tribe will be able to hold you accountable every time you don't show up that way. For instance, at the end of the meeting, ask your accountability partner how you showed up. Did you show up as Michele Obama or Wendy Williams? Two very distinct brands on two different platforms. In my own life, I've had a few moments where my brand strayed. Instead of being motivating and inspiring, I became confrontational and difficult. My accountability partner quickly gave me the feedback, "Andrea, you had a Wendy Williams moment today." This one statement allowed me to quickly self-assess and correct my course before my brand took a wrong turn.

3. Show Up with Intention Every Day

When you come into the office, be mindful of how you can use your brand story as a guide for everything you do. If your brand is around collaboration and creativity, look for opportunities to show those qualities in interactions with colleagues and customers. If your brand is creativity, find ways to be innovative in how you approach tasks. This also means getting the job done with excellence. As Steve Jobs said, "People don't know what they want until you show it to them." This requires staying on brand and consistently delivering excellence with every task. Become very intentional about how you will complete projects and deliver high-quality work every time. This also gives you the ability to get creative with brand delivery. Whether it's in the way you present a project or finding new innovative ways to approach a problem, find ways to bring your brand story to life in the workplace. Innovative thinking and creativity will help your brand story come alive, making it more memorable for colleagues and employers.

4. Leverage Social Media

Social media is a powerful tool to build brand awareness and establish yourself as a leader within your field or industry. Leverage social media channels like LinkedIn, Twitter, and Instagram to post content consistent with your brand story. When posting on social media, don't forget that you are a brand. Also, don't forget that you have a career image to protect. Keep postings professional, and engage in meaningful conversations around topics related to your brand.

As an HR professional for over 20 years, I can't tell you how many times someone has come into my office with a picture of someone's social media posts on their phone. I have also been on the receiving end of this with someone sharing my posts with my boss or other leaders within the organization.

I remember once posting something political on my social media. My mentor and accountability partner both called me immediately to remind me of my brand. They asked me, "Is this what you want to be known for? You know that post may show up again later. Are you comfortable with that?" Those simple reminders allowed me to quickly course-correct and decide whether I wanted that brand association or not. Leverage social media channels as another place to ensure your brand story is consistent and strong. In the words of my mentor, "you are not a news reporter." Very simply put, don't damage your brand by posting on things that have nothing to do with you. Now, this doesn't mean you can't share your personality and things that are important to you. It just means you must say it in a way that aligns with your brand.

So How Do You Leverage Social Media to Empower and Grow Your Brand?

First and foremost, go through your past social media posts and delete anything damaging to your brand. Going forward, at least three times a week, make posts about you and your areas of expertise. If you are in sales, your posts should show you as the best salesperson ever. Give tips on sales strategies and techniques. If you are in customer service, your posts should show you are a customer advocate and successful leader. Share stories of how you helped customers in a meaningful way. These are just two examples, but whatever your brand story is, make sure it shows up in your social media posts.

LinkedIn is a great place to post content that is brand-focused and industry related. A lot of times, people will post questions looking for solutions or helpful tips on how to handle certain situations. When you see these types of posts, take the opportunity to comment with your brand story in mind. Share your thoughts on the best solution as well as your brand story. Many recruiters and hiring managers use LinkedIn to find potential candidates, so make sure your brand story shines through when engaging in conversations about industry-related topics.

The key takeaway is that social media can be used to help tell and grow your brand story if it's done right. Find ways to engage in things relevant to your brand and create a brand story that attracts the attention of employers. You might even consider writing articles or starting a newsletter on LinkedIn.

Expand Your Brand within the Industry

The final step is to expand your brand within your industry. When you use your brand story within the company and on social media, your influence grows. As a final step, become strategic about growing your brand outside your current company but within your industry.

What activities can you do to further your story and make a name for yourself?

- Attend conferences and events to network with other key industry players.
- Read articles from thought leaders so that you have something relevant to add to meetings.
- Reach out to people who inspire you and ask questions about their career journey.
- Get a mentor whose title is at least two levels ahead of you.
- Start your own blog or podcast and share your story with the world.

Connecting with those who can help you achieve your career goals and grow your brand story is important. They will also become part of your story.

You never know how far your story can go when you share it with the right people. They will help bring your story to life. Expanding your brand within your industry makes you an expert, and you become an influencer within it.

Telling Your Story Every Day

By following these important strategies, you can start crafting your career's brand story and putting it into action, at work and in the world. Start living out your story now and watch as amazing things happen. Yours could be the inspiration for somebody else's story.

By putting your brand story into action, the right people and opportunities may come your way. So tell your story every day, and be intentional about it. Put it into action and watch how it grows and expands.

Keep pushing forward, and never give up on your story.

As the saying goes, "Your story is always writing itself." So make sure you show up each day to create the story you want to tell.

Chapter 11

When Your Brand Needs to Pivot

When everything around you changes, you gotta change to adapt. Either you pivot and profit from the change, or you procrastinate and are forced to change eventually. And when you're forced to change, there's usually a loss not a profit."

~ Hendrith Vanlon Smith Jr.

You have identified your unique strengths and potential, so how do you ensure that your brand matures while remaining true to yourself? Your brand story is never-ending. As long as you're breathing, your brand should grow. But what if you find yourself in a situation where your skills and abilities don't seem to match where your career is headed?

Meet Kendra

Kendra was a sales supervisor who loved her job. Her team's performance consistently ranked within the top ten percent of the division, and her employee engagement scores were among the top in the company. After identifying her genius and fully engaging in her DISC "SI" style, Kendra's brand story came alive. Kendra loved planning events for the team and could be counted on to send handwritten birthday notes for employees' birthdays, anniversaries, etc. While Kendra's brand was clear and valuable, it wasn't getting her promoted. Her colleagues cherished her, yet beyond the division, nobody had a clue who she was. During a chat with her boss, Kendra realized that the growth of her brand had plateaued. While she was a valuable team member, somehow, she had become known as the "good host," the "party planner," and nothing more.

Kendra realized she had spent time and energy organizing events and planning celebrations to empower the team but kept her career at a standstill. It was time to evolve. Kendra thought she only had two options. She could continue doing what she loved or stop planning events and parties and focus on getting promoted. However, the answer lies somewhere in between.

It's Time to Pivot

This is a crossroads every leader comes to. You will come to a point where your brand needs to pivot. Most leaders are tempted to pivot to the wrong space. Leaders often make the mistake of watching and imitating people recently promoted or people who seem to have the most power within the leadership team. If you want to progress your career, attempting to mimic others will not get you far. Although imitation may be the sincerest form of flattery, it won't help you expand and develop professionally. Instead of following the crowd, blaze your own trail by leveraging and maximizing your gifts and talents, going above and beyond what you would typically do.

Kendra knew it was time to pivot her brand story in a way that would reward her efforts with long-term success. She started by returning to basics—focusing on her core values, strengths, and the unique set of skills that made her team successful.

The first benefit of a great brand story is that your brand should gain visibility. Kendra's brand was only visible to her current department. When your brand reaches a plateau, always go back to the beginning and assess where you want to go.

Kendra's Pivot

Kendra was endlessly passionate about event planning and expressing gratitude to her team, yet she realized that without the right recognition, these efforts would not secure her a promotion. The goal was to get more visibility within the organization.

Kendra decided to pivot from "good host" to "go-to sales expert." Instead of planning birthday celebrations, she delegated those events over to a team member and took her skills to a new level. She became the planner of sales training, network building, and customer engagement sessions. She turned her event planning skills into sales coaching and gained the recognition and visibility she wanted.

Kendra found a way to grow while staying true to herself. She was able to pivot her brand story to get noticed by the right people, which ultimately helped her secure a promotion.

Kendra's story reminds us that we often get stuck in the same place if we keep doing what we've always done. The secret to success lies in pivoting and finding new ways to express our unique gifts and talents. We can break through the plateau and reach new heights by embracing our individuality and leveraging our strengths. That's how we make our mark in this world. Kendra discovered her genius and pursued it, which ultimately led to a promotion. Her story inspires us to believe that, with focus and dedication, anything is possible. Reach for the stars; you never know what you may find!

When your brand needs to pivot, the goal is not to do something different; it's to push forward and give your brand a new challenge. Pivoting means growing in a new direction. It means getting outside of your comfort zone and taking risks. It's about stepping out of your old ways and into a world of possibilities. That is how Kendra was able to catapult her career to the next level—she didn't do what everyone else was doing; she did something different. Kendra embraced her own genius and embraced growth.

You can do the same. Step out of your comfort zone and take risks. Let go of what's comfortable and find something new. Embrace growth and discover your genius. So take a chance on yourself; that is how Kendra became successful. Reach for the stars, and you never know what you may find.

Pivot your brand story and live life to its fullest potential!

Chapter 12
Brand Partnerships

"Talent wins games, but teamwork and intelligence win championships."
~ Michael Jordan

Serena Williams, Cardi B., Jennifer Aniston, Lady Gaga, Jamie Foxx, Alicia Keys, and Pete Davidson. These are all celebrities in their own right but have also formed brand partnerships. Brand partnerships happen when two brands align their core values and promote each other, typically in exchange for money. When it comes to your career, forming brand partnerships looks the same, except instead of money being exchanged, it's expertise and influence. A brand partnership is a great way to get your name out there, connect with like-minded professionals, and work with bigger organizations.

Every year, you should give thought to who you want to partner with, selecting three or four people who will commit to working with you to grow your career while also growing their career. These people have a great brand themselves and are also looking for ways to increase their influence and scope of work. Remember, the people you align yourself with can greatly impact your success, so pick wisely and look for shared values. They will become your brand team—the people who make you look good.

To form effective brand partnerships, you need these four people on your brand team:

Mentor

A mentor is someone who can provide you with guidance, advice, and support in your career journey—someone who has been there and done it all before. This person will help keep you on track and challenged to reach your highest potential. They should have a proven track record of success and be able to bring an external perspective to your work. It's a mentor's role to help you see things forward, guide you, and offer advice based on their experience. A mentor should work with you on a few very specific goals; it shouldn't be an exhaustive list. Your mentor should be someone whose title is no more than two levels above you and who also has a great brand story.

You may have more than one mentor, but each one should guide you in different career areas. For example, you may have a mentor within your organization who can help you navigate its landscape. Your company mentor may be able to work with you on becoming more visible within the organization, helping you through internal leadership challenges as they come up.

You may also have a mentor who is outside of your organization. This mentor could be in a different industry or one who has mastered the art of networking and can provide valuable insights you wouldn't get from someone inside your organization. This mentor may partner with you on expanding your brand outside the organization by helping you network within the industry or become more visible through speaking engagements.

Peer Partnership

A peer brand partnership is one of the greatest partnerships. Look for a peer who is on the fast track within the company. This person should have the same values and goals as you but may be slightly ahead of you in terms of success. This person is invaluable because they can offer you great insight into navigating the waters of your company and help you find out who is who and what opportunities exist. It's also important that this peer has a good brand story and is a great connector.

Mentee

You also need to form a mentee brand partnership. This is where you become a mentor for someone else. This is an opportunity for you to give back and have a lasting impact on someone else's career. A mentee should be someone who is at least one level below you in title but has strong potential, ambition and drive. You can help guide this person through their own career journey by helping them grow, develop, problem-solve, and navigate the waters of your organization. When you become a mentor for someone else, they become your brand ambassador.

Sponsor

A sponsor has influence and power in the organization or the industry. This individual can and will advocate for you, opening doors to opportunities that may not have been available without them. They should be more senior than your mentor but still accessible and willing to help you grow. Your sponsor will help elevate your visibility. They will also be the voice in the room when you are not present. Remember, your brand story speaks long after you've left the room. With a sponsor on your brand team, they will be the voice that speaks positively about you in every room. With a brand sponsor on your team, you are introducing a powerful advocate to your brand story who can support you and help further your career.

What's in It for You—and Them?

The word partnership implies a two-way relationship, and a brand partnership should be no different. Each partner should get something out of it. For example, you may offer your mentor insight into how Millennials perceive current trends or what's happening in the workplace right now. Your peer can benefit from your expertise and knowledge as well as gain insight into how to be a successful leader. Your mentee can gain invaluable knowledge and skills from you that may not otherwise be accessible to them. And finally, your sponsor can benefit from having their name attached to a rising star in the organization or industry.

With each of these brand partnerships, it's important to remember that the relationship should be mutually beneficial. Everyone should get something out of it, and the partnership should not be one-sided. Your brand partnerships are essential in helping you build a strong personal and professional brand because they provide avenues to help you grow, learn, and succeed. When you do it right, there is no limit to what you can achieve with a strong team of brand partners behind you.

Most importantly, a brand partnership helps each person's brand become bigger, better, and stronger. Your reputation is on the line, and so are the reputations of those partnered with you. Brand partnerships are a great way to build relationships, create opportunities and reach new levels of success. So don't take them lightly. Find the right partners, nurture the relationships, and watch your brand grow!

I'm sure you now understand why it's crucial to develop strong brand partnerships. Take some time to think about who you can bring into your team and what roles they need to play.

Building effective brand partnerships will take time and commitment, but it's worth it in the long run. Finding like-minded professionals that share similar values can be an invaluable asset and can help you reach greater heights. Think carefully about who you want on your brand team, and make sure to find people who have similar goals and ambitions. With the right mix of skills and personalities, these four people can become invaluable allies in your career journey.

My Brand Partnerships

I have had the pleasure of creating brand partnerships with four very special people. When my career took an unexpected turn in the form of a company reorganization, my brand partnerships were key to the next level of my success. Several years ago, I met a leader at a networking event. Throughout the years, we stayed in touch and agreed we really wanted to work together in some way. When I was ready to launch my coaching business full-time, he was the person I called for support. Now, he is the official sponsor of my business and has helped me build a strong presence within the consulting industry.

My second partnership is a peer within the coaching industry. We connected through a network of coaches and have agreed to come together and help each other succeed. While we are both coaches, we are not in competition with each other. Instead, we promote one another's businesses. You will often see me posting about her events, and she has been a huge supporter of my books, sharing tips from them on her website.

My latest partnership is with a local brand photographer. We connected when I saw her work on an Instagram post and reached out to her. We exchanged ideas and collaborated on a very successful project. She has become my go-to photographer for headshots, photoshoots, social media content, and marketing projects. In return, I promote her photography skills and refer my tribe to her whenever I can.

Who can you form a partnership with to increase your brand awareness? Take some time to think about who would make a great partner and what they can bring to the table. Be sure to find someone with shared values, complementary skill sets, and even similar goals. When done correctly, brand partnerships can be vital in helping you reach greater heights.

With every brand partnership, you have the opportunity to grow, learn, and succeed. Don't take this lightly; create strong relationships with those you partner with, nurture the relationship, and watch your brand reach its highest potential. Brand partnerships should never be one-sided—make sure both parties benefit from the partnership, as this will make it successful in the long run. Find a brand partner who can help you move forward and reach your goals. Together, you'll create a successful partnership that will benefit both parties.

Chapter 13
Haters, Trolls, and Detractors

"Haters will fail, if you stay focused."
~ Tyler Perry

A lot of successful companies have what's called a Net Promoter Score. This score is calculated by subtracting the number of people who like and support a company from the number of people who don't. Although it's nice to have as many supporters as possible, having detractors can be just as important.

Detractors are those who actively speak out against you or your product in public forums or social media channels. They may not like your product or service, and they will likely be vocal in their criticism. Despite the negative attention haters bring, they can actually serve an important purpose—they can provide valuable feedback on areas where improvements could be made. If you listen closely, there's often a kernel of truth in what detractors have to say.

When it comes to your brand story, you will have people who don't like you. I call them haters, trolls, and detractors. I know it may be hard to believe, but when it comes to your career, you will definitely have them.

Haters are people who don't appreciate your brand story because they disagree with it or simply don't find it interesting. These people will say negative things about you and even deliberately spread malicious rumors about you. Have you ever had someone on your team that just doesn't like you? They use every opportunity to make you look bad in meetings? This person is a hater. Haters are often jealous and insecure and will never be happy for your success. These can be people who have been with the company for many years and are unhappy. They don't want to grow in their career, and they don't want you to grow, either. The thing to remember with haters is your growth will always upset them. Your growth is the reminder that success is possible.

Trolls are those people who watch your career like a hawk. They will never give you kudos or a compliment. They take every opportunity to criticize your work, even when you do something great. These people are rarely successful in their own right and will always make sure to put you down so that they can feel better about themselves. Trolls often hide in the shadows, but if you watch closely, you will see who they are. Think about the social media trolls, those people who create fake profiles to make negative comments. Trolls are everywhere, and they have no problem bringing you down to make themselves feel better.

Detractors are those who actively speak out against you. This could be a peer, a boss or even someone who has not interacted much with you. They are not really haters and not trolls. The difference is that a detractor has had some interaction with you. Perhaps they had a disagreement with you, and now they are out to discredit your work. Maybe you worked together on a project that didn't go so well. Detractors will always tell one story about one time they interacted with you. They can be vocal about their opinion, and it can affect your career.

So how do you handle haters, trolls and detractors?

My mom has the best advice when it comes to this subject. Her advice: what you don't feed will die. In other words, don't give haters, trolls and detractors any attention. Ignore them, and they will go away. This is easier said than done, but it's the best way to handle these situations.

The key is to remain focused on your goals and be confident in yourself. Don't let anyone tell you that you can't succeed. Stay positive, and don't let the negativity get you down. Don't be afraid to stand up for yourself, either. Your goal is not to change their minds about you. It's not important that you change a hater into a friend or a troll into a fan. You do not have to make a detractor a promoter of your brand. The only strategy you need is to drown out their narrative. And the way to do this is to continue to grow your brand and gain enough supporters and raging fans that their voice becomes silent.

Ultimately, you have to remember that haters, trolls and detractors are not in control of your career. You are, and your success is up to you. As long as you focus on building a strong brand story and getting people behind it, the noise from the haters, trolls and detractors will decrease. So don't let the negativity get you down; stay focused on your goals and continue to move forward. You got this!

The other important thing to remember is that haters, trolls and detractors can actually serve an important purpose—they can provide valuable feedback on areas where improvements may need to be made. If you listen closely, there's often a kernel of wisdom in their criticism. If your detractor has worked with you on a project or you've had an argument, there is likely something to be learned from that experience. By taking a step back and looking at the situation objectively, you may gain valuable insight into improving your approach—or even yourself. If your haters are vocal about something that you know is wrong, you have good reason to challenge them.

At the end of the day, it's important to remember that haters, trolls and detractors are part of life. But don't let their negativity bring you down or define your success. Take haters, trolls and detractors with a grain of salt. The key is to remain focused on your goals and be confident in yourself. Don't let anyone tell you that you can't succeed. With the right attitude, a little bit of knowledge, and taking action, you can and will prove your haters wrong!

Chapter 14
When Your Brand Takes a Wrong Turn

"It takes 20 years to build a reputation and five minutes to ruin it. If you think about that, you'll do things differently."
~ Warren Buffett

On September 17, 1983, 20-year-old Vanessa Williams became the first African American to be crowned Miss America. In July of 1984, just two months before the end of her rein her brand story changed. Williams was forced to relinquish her crown after nude photos of her taken several years prior surfaced.

The scandal caused an uproar and national media coverage ensued. Williams was publicly shamed and vilified by many. It seemed like her career as a public figure was finished, but that wasn't the case.

No matter how much work you do to create your brand and tell your brand story, inevitably, there will be times when your brand takes a wrong turn. Whether it's an unanticipated mistake, a failure, a rumor that tarnishes your reputation, or haters looking to tear you down on social media, there are steps you can take to restore your brand after misfortunes and strengthen it for the future.

I believe your brand can and probably will take a hit in three categories: mistakes, misses and unexpected challenges.

Mistakes

As you grow, there will be times when you make mistakes. It could be a missed deadline, a data calculation error, or something you said in a meeting that didn't land how you intended. Mistakes happen. Everyone makes mistakes, and you will be no different. The key is to learn from them, understand what went wrong, and take steps to ensure it doesn't happen again. Also, own your mistakes. People have very long memories but are quick to forgive when you own your mistakes. When it comes to your brand story, there will be mistakes, and those mistakes will also become part of your brand story. So in the same breath that someone talks about your mistakes, they should also tell the story of your resilience and how you overcame them.

Misses

Misses happen when something falls short of expectation. This could be a time when you gave it your all but came up short. It could be a time when you simply missed the mark. Whatever the reason, it's important to take some time to reflect on what happened and how you can learn from it. No one enjoys missing their mark, but taking the time to learn will strengthen your brand story in the future and show your resilience. In my own career, I've had many misses. I've missed the mark by arguing for the wrong thing, by not listening to my team or customers, and in many other cases.

Unexpected Challenges

Unexpected challenges can come out of nowhere and shake up your brand story. It could be an unexpected pandemic or the loss of a family member. Or you could be like Vanessa Williams, and have something from your past overshadow your current brand story. I once had the pleasure of coaching a leader whose past mistakes as a troubled teenager came rushing into his brand story. Someone from his former life was happy to share the mistakes he'd made over fifteen years ago with his new employer.

How do you recover from mistakes, misses and unexpected challenges?

Before you do anything, fully assess the circumstances. Breathe and take the time to understand what happened and why. Take a few days or even weeks to sit with the challenge before rushing into any decisions.

Then, plan your response. Come up with an actionable plan that will help you move forward. Talk to your trusted tribe, your brand partners, and mentors and get their perspectives. Not only will this help you put together a plan of action, it can also provide the much-needed emotional support to keep you going.

Again, acknowledge mistakes and own your misses. Apologize if necessary, and be transparent with your audience about what happened and why. Show people how you've learned from the situation, addressed any issues, and strengthened your brand story moving forward.

The best brand strategy for recovering from a wrong turn is to openly share what you've learned and include it in your brand story. This could look like writing a quick article or newsletter or blog post. You can share your story, your way, controlling the narrative. I've had to do this many times in my own career brand story. I've given speeches and inspirational talks using my misses and failures.

In the case of Vanessa Williams, she was able to successfully recover her brand. Instead of letting the scandal define her, she chose to rise above it and rebuild her image. She took responsibility for her actions, apologized publicly, and worked hard to regain trust and respect from those who had been affected by her mistake.

The final step in recovering from a wrong turn is to move on. Don't dwell on the past, and don't allow a mistake or miss to define you and your brand story.

Just because your brand takes a wrong turn doesn't mean it's the end of the world, and it's certainly not the end of your career.

Just like Vanessa Williams, there will come a time when that mistake is just one line in your story. It won't define you; it will show just how resilient you can be.

The key is to stay focused on the big picture and remember that, even in our darkest moments, we have the power to write our own stories. So take time to grieve and assess, but don't forget to keep pushing forward until you reach your destination. The future of your brand depends on it.

Chapter 15
Staying In Your Lane

"Stay in your car in your lane on your road in your world. Stay in your own lane. Don't be minding other people's spiritual business. Stay in your car. In your lane. On your road. In your world."
~ Iyanla Vanzant

You've done the hard but fun work of defining your brand story. The challenge you will face time and time again, is to remember to stay in your lane. You must stay true to your brand and your unique brand story.

The old saying goes, "Imitation is the sincerest form of flattery," yet this adage could not be further from reality when it comes to advancing your professional career. Frequently, we observe a person who has recently been promoted and feel inspired to emulate their success.

Meet Lisa

Lisa was a young professional who had achieved some success in the corporate world but was feeling the itch to move up the ladder of success. She was constantly watching her peers and eagerly attempting to follow their steps, no matter how divergent they were from her goals and values.

As Lisa continued to focus on mimicking those around her, she became increasingly frustrated and confused. She was not enjoying the work she was doing and often felt overwhelmed because her efforts were not successful and did not produce the desired results. In fact, the quality of her work began to suffer.

Finally, Lisa had an epiphany; she needed to focus on her own strengths and stop pressuring herself to be something or someone she was not. She began to pay more attention to what inspired her personally and professionally.

As a result of focusing on her unique brand story, Lisa discovered that by staying in her lane, she was able to be her very best. Her enthusiasm and passion for her work began to grow, and she was producing more creative solutions than ever before.

The moral of Lisa's story is simple: never forget the power of staying in your lane and honoring your own brand story. Staying true to yourself will help you achieve success faster and with greater satisfaction. Don't be intimidated by the perceived success of those around you; focus on your own journey, and trust that if you stay in your lane, great things will come to pass.

The Reality of Imitation: A Recipe for Failure

Rather than taking cues from those around us, we must take our own advice and remain true to ourselves. Learning from the successes and failures of others is an effective way to gain knowledge, but it should not be used as a crutch for our own success.

By staying in your lane, you are honoring your brand story. You are taking ownership of who you are and what you believe in—no matter how different it may be from someone else. The key to remember is that your brand makes you an original, not a carbon copy. Karen may have been recently promoted, and she is a rockstar in analyzing data and forecasting trends. But, to be brutally honest, there is already a Karen on the team, and it doesn't need an imitation. That is not to say that you can't learn from her success or capture elements of it for yourself, but it does mean that the way you do this must be suitable to your own skills and values.

The Rewards of Staying in Your Lane

When we honor our brand story, we become empowered and begin to understand our skills and values in a deeper way. We become more comfortable with taking risks and we learn how to own up to our successes and failures.

Most importantly, when we stay in our lane, it allows us to express ourselves fully in a unique way that cannot be replicated by anyone else. It gives us an opportunity to stand out and become the person that others look up to as an example of how we can all reach our highest potential.

By staying in your lane, you are honoring your brand story and taking ownership of who you are and what you believe in. Take the time to explore what makes you unique and don't be afraid to take risks. The rewards are worth it!

Chapter 16
Danger: The Four Killers of Your Brand

"Often those that criticise others reveal what he himself lacks."
~ Shannon L. Alder

Creating and maintaining the brand you create is not always easy.

When you start thinking of yourself as a brand, your career will grow organically. Your brand will put you in different rooms with a variety of people. The more you grow, the more your brand grows. One of the worse things you can do is spend time creating a brand and then destroying it. It's much easier to destroy a brand than it is to create one.

Meet Tami

Tami had been with the company for about seven years. She planned to finish her degree and move up in the organization. The minute she finished her degree, she began creating her brand story. And her story was a great one. Once a month, the company would host what was known as General Information Sessions. This is where the company would open its doors, hosting a job fair highlighting all its open positions. On the advice of a great career coach (in case you're wondering, it's me), Tami asked her boss if she could help at an upcoming session. She was excited to share her success story; she was a walking billboard for the company.

Tami attended the General Information Session and told her story so compellingly that potential candidates were flocking to join the organization. The next day, Tami received a call from the director of the talent team, offering her a job as a recruiter. Tami jumped at the opportunity and began her new role shortly thereafter.

Her joy was short-lived. Within a few months, Tami went from the company's poster child to a pariah. The company's leadership considered Tami to be the prime example of how not to grow your career. How did it happen?

Tami was guilty of becoming one of the four brand killers.

Gossiping

Nothing destroys your credibility like gossiping or talking about others behind their back. This can ruin relationships with co-workers, customers and even employers—instantly!

To fit in with her new coworkers, Tami began hanging out at a local pub after work with her co-workers. One too many glasses of pinot grigio and Tami was laughing and joining in on conversations about her boss, other employees, and even customers. This weekly hang-out continued for a few months, and while Tami was the life of the party, her reputation in the company was suffering. Eventually, someone told her boss what was going on, and Tami's brand tanked.

The moral of the story: When you think of yourself as your own brand, be mindful of your actions, words, and behavior so that it doesn't negatively affect how others perceive you. Gossiping can be especially damaging to your career because it's difficult to undo your words once they've been said. Stay focused on building relationships and providing value in order to grow professionally!

Gossiping isn't the only brand killer to worry about, though. There are three others to watch out for too.

People Pleasing

There is nothing wrong with striving for excellence, but there *is* something wrong when you constantly give in to people's demands to please them. Doing this compromises your integrity and does not make you a reliable professional. What is people pleasing exactly? People pleasing is when you put yourself in a position of always trying to make everyone around you happy. So that you don't rock the boat, you agree with everyone, even those ideas you don't agree with. You may find yourself feeling like you can't say no to anyone's requests. Doing this takes away from the true value that you bring to the table. Being a people pleaser will kill your brand because it devalues your gifts, skills and talents.

Being a people pleaser has many detrimental effects on your professional integrity and career growth. It can lead to feelings of resentment, stress, and burnout since you're constantly putting other people's needs before your own. By trying to keep everyone happy, you may compromise your own values and standards by doing things that you don't necessarily agree with, simply because someone else asked you to do it. This can lead to a lack of personal fulfillment and may even result in sacrificing progress toward bigger goals or dreams.

Furthermore, trying to always please everyone can make you appear unreliable or untrustworthy since they never truly know where your loyalties lie. Your peers might start to doubt your judgment if they see that you are always second-guessing yourself or giving in to what others want instead of taking the initiative. You may be seen as an indecisive or weak leader who doesn't have their own opinion as opposed to a strong independent voice who stands up for themselves and their opinions.

Being a people pleaser could tarnish your reputation in the workplace as someone who is only interested in appeasing those around them rather than producing meaningful work that serves the greater good of the team or organization. People may not appreciate your efforts if you take action out of fear or coercion rather than genuine interest in achieving results and making meaningful contributions. In short, being a people pleaser can hinder both personal growth and professional success.

There are 4 things that can easily destroy your hard-earned brand: gossiping, people pleasing, being the go-to guy and becoming a Jack of all trades. Each one of these can have negative consequences that do not always show up immediately but become realized over time.

Gossiping is something we should all avoid as much as possible. While it may be tempting to join in on some juicy conversation, resist and focus on building relationships with people you trust and respect instead. Gossip will eventually come back around to you or someone else, damaging your reputation in the process.

People pleasing is also dangerous when it comes to growing your brand. It's easy to say yes to everyone, but when you do this, you take away from the unique value you bring. It's ok to say no occasionally and be selective about who and what you commit to.

The "Go-To Person"

Being the "go-to guy/gal" is a trap many fall into. This is a mistake many first-time leaders fall into, and they never quite make it out again.

Being the go-to guy can have a negative effect on your career for many reasons. Firstly, taking on every problem and task that comes your way can be overwhelming. It can lead to burnout, fatigue, and exhaustion if you aren't mindful of your own energy and limits. Additionally, taking on too much responsibility may prevent you from exploring other areas within the company or developing new skills. These issues could limit your career growth and advancement opportunities.

It is also important to consider how others perceive you when you always step up to the plate. While it's admirable to be willing to help out in a pinch, it can also pigeonhole you into a certain role and make it more difficult for others to trust or rely on your judgment if they know they can always count on you to do something. This could lead people to view you as a pushover rather than someone with their own opinions or insights.

Finally, being the go-to guy may cause resentment from coworkers who feel like they never get recognition for their contributions compared to those who seem to be constantly in the spotlight due to their willingness and ability to take on extra tasks. This could lead people to feel unappreciated, and they may be reluctant or unwilling to work together as a team since everyone is constantly competing for attention or trying not fall behind.

The Jack of All Trades is the Master of None

The last brand killer is becoming a Jack of All Trades. This is a sneaky brand killer, especially if you are gifted at strategy. A Jack of All Trades can do multiple things and handle multiple projects. This is the person leaders call on when there's something nobody else wants to take on. Sorry, but it's true. If you are the person who gets handed various projects that do not align with your brand, you are a Jack of All Trades, and your brand is in serious jeopardy.

Being a Jack of All Trades, or JAT, can have many negative effects on personal growth and professional success. When an individual attempts to become accomplished in multiple fields without truly mastering any of them, it can lead to decreased expertise in each area. This lack of specialization often leads to a lack of recognition from peers and supervisors, making it difficult for JATs to be rewarded for their efforts. Furthermore, attempting to take on too much at once can lead to burnout due to the multiple demands placed on the individual. The inability to commit enough time and focus on one particular task or career could overwhelm and discourage them from achieving their goals. Ultimately, becoming a Jack of All Trades can also put JATs at risk of becoming complacent and not staying up-to-date with industry trends or changes. As such, they may miss out on new opportunities that require specialized skillsets and knowledge they don't possess because they haven't committed enough time to hone those abilities. Therefore, if you want to stand out professionally and reach your highest potential, you must focus on specializing in your superpower, your unique genius. The only projects and assignments that should come your way should be the ones that focus on your strengths and what you do best. Don't be afraid to say no when something doesn't align with your brand and focus. Your personal brand is too important to risk. Keep it strong and protect it at all costs. Remember, less is more! Be a master of one rather than a Jack of All Trades!

It is essential to establish and maintain a strong personal brand that aligns with the skillsets you possess. By not becoming a gossiper, people pleaser, go-to guy/gal or Jack of All Trades, you can ensure your reputation remains intact while also protecting yourself from burnout due to taking on too much at once. Cultivating an authentic professional image will open more doors for career growth opportunities and help ensure that everyone knows what makes you unique and special within any organization. So stay focused on specializing in your superpower—your unique genius—and don't be afraid to say no when something doesn't align with your brand goals!

Chapter 17
Know When to Leave the Party

"If you're brave enough to say goodbye, life will reward you with a new hello."
~ Paulo Coelho

You've done the work of growing your brand and having a stellar brand story. People are saying great things about you. You've experienced growth within the company, taken on additional projects, and may have been promoted once or twice. But now there's no room for the next promotion. Let's face it; there's only one CEO of the company. The higher up you go in title, the fewer opportunities for promotion.

It's like being at a party for too long. The people are leaving; the DJ has started packing up his equipment. The music has stopped, but you're still there trying to dance. Believe me, I've been there.

I greatly admire the Millennials' ability to know when it's time to leave the party. If you understand that your brand has outgrown the company and there are no more ideas on how to continue making progress within it, then it might be a good idea to look for new opportunities.

There's nothing wrong with looking for new opportunities. It's actually a sign of growth and maturity, not weakness. Think about it this way; you're permitting yourself to be the best version of you by allowing yourself to explore the world outside your current boundaries.

Recently, the best tech companies have begun layoffs. It definitely happens. I have been on the receiving end of a layoff conversation more than once in my career.

Even the best companies might have to let go of their best employees for one reason or another.

There's a song in the Broadway play *Hamilton* that says:

No one really knows how the game is played

The art of the trade

How the sausage gets made

We just assume that it happens

But no one else is in the room where it happens

You never know how the layoff game is played. Yes, you could be a top performer, adding value to the organization. But behind those closed corporate doors, in the room where layoffs and restructures are discussed, you very well might find yourself the victim of a dismissal.

Listen, I get it. You love the company, and your boss is terrific to work with. All your work BFFs are there, and you don't want to leave. That's how everyone should feel every day of their career. However, if the company shifts, your great boss leaves, or your work BFFs all resign, you have to be prepared. Even when you love your job, you have to remember it's your career, and you are the one who's always in control.

As you grow your brand and your brand story gets bigger and better, you may find yourself at a crossroads, asking yourself, "Do I stay or do I go?"

If you love the company, and the company's brand still aligns with your brand, you could very well stay. Just know the longer you stay, the less money you will earn. Why do I say this?

I have observed top performers who had been consistently rated as highly effective and outstanding over four to six years; Each performance appraisal was associated with a larger salary rise. From these observations, I can confidently conclude that after several years of such commendable service, employees will become exceedingly well-paid. In some cases, they may even reach the ceiling of their respective pay grades. What happens next? They become stagnant, and with their over-inflated salary, they are deemed too expensive to promote.

If you find yourself in a situation like this, remember that your brand story is still intact; it's just time for you to look for opportunities elsewhere.

Exploring New Opportunities

When you realize the music has stopped playing, and it may be time to leave the party, take your time and do your due diligence.

Stealth Mode

Stealth mode means going about your job search without any of your current employers or colleagues knowing. This is not the time to share information with your beloved boss or work BFF. Why? Because it could put your current job in jeopardy. And everybody knows it's easier to find a job when you have one. You can take your time and be selective in choosing the right next opportunity.

Part of your brand story strategy was to increase your presence online using social media. Your LinkedIn presence should be on point, and if you've written articles or blog posts, they will definitely come in handy. Your online presence becomes the cover letter to your resume.

LinkedIn is the platform designed to help you keep your professional profile visible and up-to-date. It's also a great place to network, find new job opportunities, or even start building your own business. Staying active on LinkedIn keeps you updated on trends and industry news and helps you connect with potential employers. If you ever have to look for a new career opportunity, hiring managers and professional recruiters will look for you based on your LinkedIn profile.

Update Your Resume

It's essential to keep your resume up to date, especially if you're in a fast-changing industry. Make sure all your previous job experiences and accomplishments are listed accurately. It's also a good idea to make a calendar reminder to make any necessary updates to your resume every six months so that it stays fresh and relevant. Continuously update your accomplishments, projects, and skills to reflect your current experience.

Apply for Next-Level Positions Outside of the Organization

Apply for next-level positions at other companies at least twice a year, even if you plan on staying in your current job. Applying for new roles will help keep your skills sharp and ensure that you remain competitive in the job market. It also gives you an idea of where the industry is headed and what skills employers are seeking. Applying for positions at the next level will also show you what you need to do to reach your career goals. So keep your resume updated so you're always prepared for whatever comes your way!

Go on At Least Two Interviews Every Year

Interviews are an important part of the job search process. Even if you're not actively looking for a new job, it's still good practice to go on at least two interviews a year. Being intentional about interviewing will help keep your interview skills sharp and remind you of your value in the market. It also gives you valuable insight into different companies and industries, which could be helpful when it comes to making informed decisions about your career path. If you're seriously considering leaving your current job, brush up on those interview skills!

Networking Is King

Your professional network is one of your most valuable assets. It can help you land a new job or connect with potential business partners. Keep growing your network and stay in touch with professional peers, industry leaders, mentors, and other contacts. Staying involved in professional networks will also ensure you are always connected to the right people and opportunities. Join and remain active in various networks within your profession. With networking, staying on top of industry trends and building meaningful relationships is easy.

Networking also includes attending webinars, conferences, seminars, and workshops. These networking events are great places to meet new people and learn more about your profession. They also allow you to showcase your skills and knowledge to potential employers or business partners. So if a conference or workshop interests you, make sure to attend it. And if there's a Facebook or LinkedIn group within your profession, don't hesitate to join and become an active member.

Become a Subject Matter Expert

Everyone wants to find a job they love within a great organization. Employees want to grow, learn, and be successful. It's not wrong to want to stay with a company for a long, successful career. But if you stay with one company for too long, it can have serious drawbacks. So, to ensure you stay employable, it's important to become an expert in your field. This means taking courses, gaining certifications, reading related books and articles, attending seminars and workshops, and staying informed of the latest industry trends. Becoming a subject-matter expert will help keep your skills sharp and demonstrate your value as an employee or potential business partner. It will also make you more attractive to potential employers or business partners. So, if you want your career to reach the next level, strive to become an expert in your field!

Continuously Update Yourself

When it comes to career growth and development, there's no such thing as a free ride. To truly stay competitive in the job market, it's important to continuously update your skills and knowledge so you can stay ahead of the curve. This means taking courses, reading books, attending seminars, and doing anything else that will help keep your skills sharp. It also means learning new technologies as they become available and staying up-to-date on industry trends and news. By staying abreast of the latest job market trends and developments, you can ensure that your skills remain relevant and valuable. So, strive to stay current in your field and be open to learning new things!

By following these tips, you'll take control of your career development and find more success at every stage. When your brand outgrows the company, you'll be prepared to take on new challenges and opportunities. You'll also have a competitive edge that will ensure you stay employable and valuable in the job market.

Chapter 18
Brand Yourself

"Personal branding is about managing your name—even if you don't own a business—in a world of misinformation, disinformation, and semi-permanent Google records. Going on a date? Chances are that your 'blind' date has Googled your name. Going to a job interview? Ditto."
~Tim Ferriss

I will end this book the way it began.

It is called Brand Yourself Before Someone Else Does because you will find that the world is full of people creating and telling stories. We all tell everyone else's story every day. Think about how many "stories" you tell about people you don't know, celebrities, politicians, etc. You also tell them about the people you do know. You tell the brand story of that crazy coworker, the difficult boss, the smart but lazy employee, etc.

You may not realize it, but you already have a story that is being told about you. People are talking about you in your industry and probably beyond it. The question becomes, do you want to control that narrative or allow someone else to?

If you choose to take control of your narrative, then all the ideas and strategies in this book will help you create an authentic career brand story that is consistent and engaging. As long as you stay true to yourself and focus on authenticity, you can be sure that the story of your career success will be a positive one.

My final three pieces of advice:

Take Ownership of Your Brand Story

No matter how difficult the journey may be, it is important to remember that owning your brand story is an invaluable asset in your career. It allows you to define yourself and control your personal narrative. Taking ownership of your personal brand story can help you stand out from the crowd by showcasing what makes you unique as a person and a professional.

Keep Learning and Reflecting

You never want to stop growing and developing yourself professionally. Many leaders struggle because they stop learning and, ultimately, stop growing. They eventually discover, a bit too late, the industry has outpaced their growth. Let's face it; anything you don't feed will eventually die. The same holds true for your career and your own development. The best leaders are always learning, growing and trying new things. Look at Kelly Clarkson, Queen Latifah, and Richard Branson. These individuals could all have taken their one-time success and called it quits.

If you ever find yourself stuck or stalled, the first question to ask is:

What have I done in the last twelve months to grow myself? Growth is the antidote to death. Nothing can die if it's growing.

START COACHING WITH ME AND MY TEAM

The best athletes in the world have professional coaches—not to teach them how to play the game but to help them become the best. A great coach shows you how to get beyond your current level and up to the next level. They help you implement strategies to push yourself to the next level of your game. My team and I would love to be part of your journey, helping you take ownership of your brand story and reach the highest levels in your industry. Let's get started today. Book a free discovery call with one of my coaches or me.

To learn more about how you can be part of our coaching experience, visit my websites:

www.andreaoden.com

www.airnetworkllc.com

Conclusion

Thank you for joining me on this brand story journey. I hope you've learned a few things along the way. My brand story has been a game-changer in my career and has also been filled with many twists and turns. There have been days when my brand was shining bright and days when I wanted to run and hide. But the truth is, that's my story, in all of its glory and splendor. Every high and every low was the driving force behind my success. I tell the valley stories with just as much passion as I do the mountain-top highs.

My brand story has allowed me to:

- Launch a coaching business, coaching leaders throughout the United States
- Speak on stage as a motivational speaker and thought leader
- Develop a brand as being an authority for career and leadership development
- Author six books with thousands of sales
- Become a professional recruiter with a successful recruiting extension to my coaching business
- Become an HR consultant for three startup companies
- Be a trusted advisor to c-suite leaders
- Become a top LinkedIn content provider
- Be a recognized public event and keynote speaker
- Become a featured guest on podcasts
- Host and moderate industry events

Because of my brand story, clients and companies want to work with me; they feel connected to my story.

I would love to connect to your brand story. If you enjoyed this journey, put out a social media post with you holding this book and tag me—@theandreaoden—so I can get involved with your brand story.

Book Andrea Oden

If you're looking for the ultimate keynote experience, Andrea is your person. She has been consistently rated #1 by meeting planners and attendees when it comes to delivering world-class motivation packed with energy and authenticity. Her inspiring story and down-to-earth demeanor captivate her audience, creating hilarity with high energy while providing actionable strategies to help them achieve the next level of success. She is an unstoppable force in optimizing results! When booking Andrea as a speaker, she promises an entertaining journey, leaving event-goers feeling inspired long after the curtains close.

BOOK ANDREA FOR YOUR NEXT EVENT:

andreaoden.com/bookandreaoden

About the Author

Andrea Oden, a life strategist and highly sought-after keynote speaker, is also CEO of AIR Network. Her gift of transforming lives through her teaching and motivational speaking has been widely acclaimed for over 20 years.

Andrea faced many adversaries as she moved into the world of leadership, yet her faith and courage led her to break down barriers in boardrooms and churches throughout the United States. In Corporate America, she began her career as a typist. Twenty years later, she held the title of Human Resources Director within a Fortune 100 company.

In 2000, she was the first female licensed and ordained minister at New St. John Community Baptist Church in Chicago, Illinois. To this day, she holds the only license ever issued to a female from the church, but she definitely seeks to change that by equipping women to stand in their truth, power and authenticity in the boardroom and the church.

Andrea Oden is leaving an undeniable mark in the world and has a passion to multiply that mark, leaving a legacy that never ends.

Andrea lives in a Michigan Suburb with her family but calls Chicago home.

Made in the USA
Middletown, DE
08 March 2024

51012883R00051